A Home Like This

Contents

Written by Gemma Bagnall

Home Sweet Home

Some people live in a house. Some people live in a flat, or a boat! No matter where they live, it is always their home.

Lots of houses are made of bricks.
Some are made of stone, slate or wood.

Houses

Houses can stand alone or be connected. On some streets, there are two houses connected in a pair.

Many houses can be connected in a long row.

Bungalows

Some homes have no stairs. They are called bungalows.

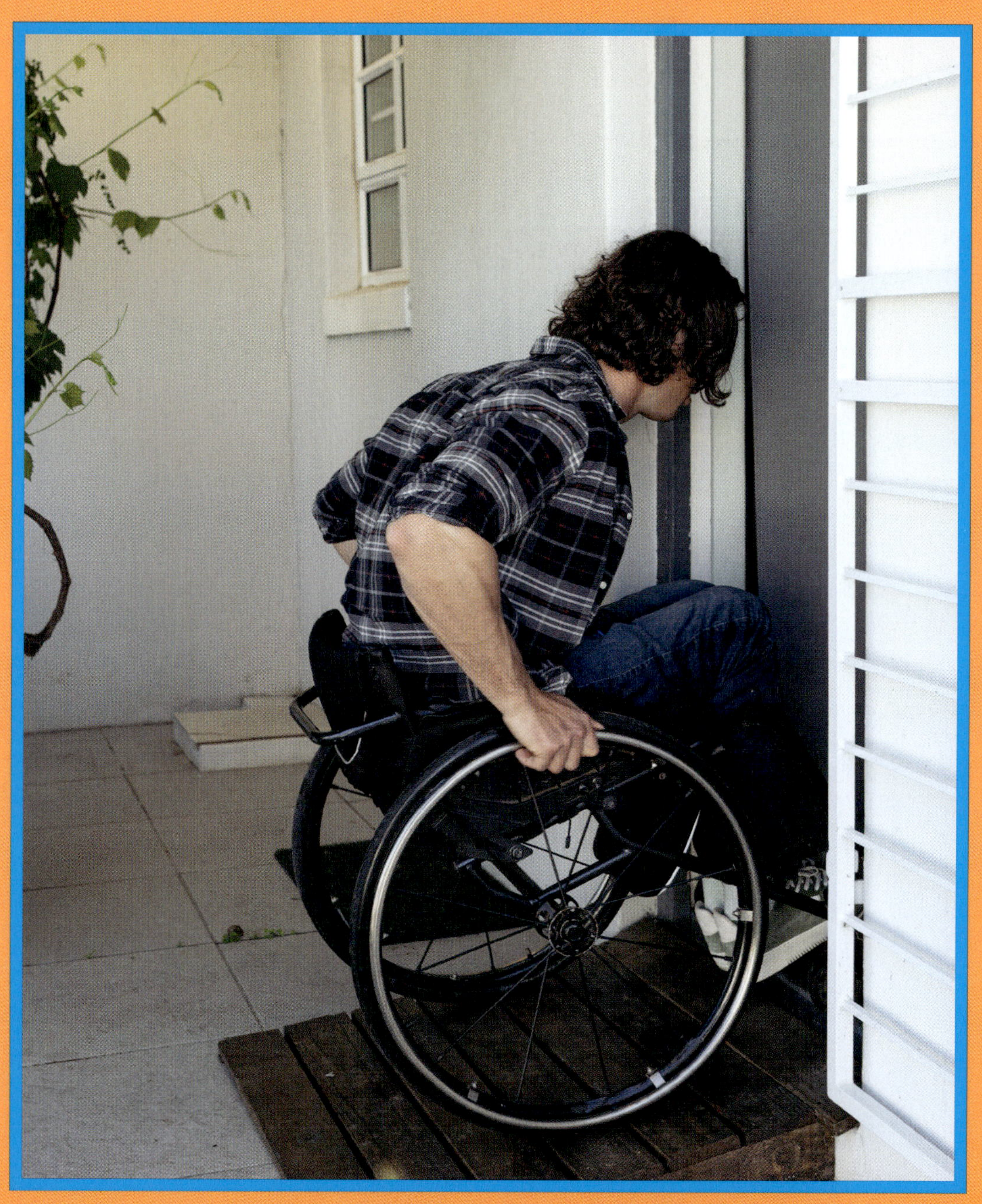

All of the rooms are at ground level.
Bungalows are great for people who find
it difficult to get upstairs.

Flats

Some homes are on different levels of the same place. This is a block of flats.

Lots of people live here. You can see for miles from the top flats!

Boats

Some homes are on water. This narrowboat
home is on a canal. You can travel around
on the canals if you like to see new places.

People who live on narrowboats might choose
to stay in the same place a lot of the time.

Caravans

Some homes are trailers or caravans. This is a Traveller site, where lots of families live.

On the site, there is space for children to ride their bikes and play.

Army Homes

This home is on an army base. People in the army can live here with their families.

Some families might not stay at the same base. They may have to travel to different bases all over the globe!

What a Home!

There are many different kinds of homes. Would you like to live in a home like this?